KU-395-806

ACC. No: 02985228

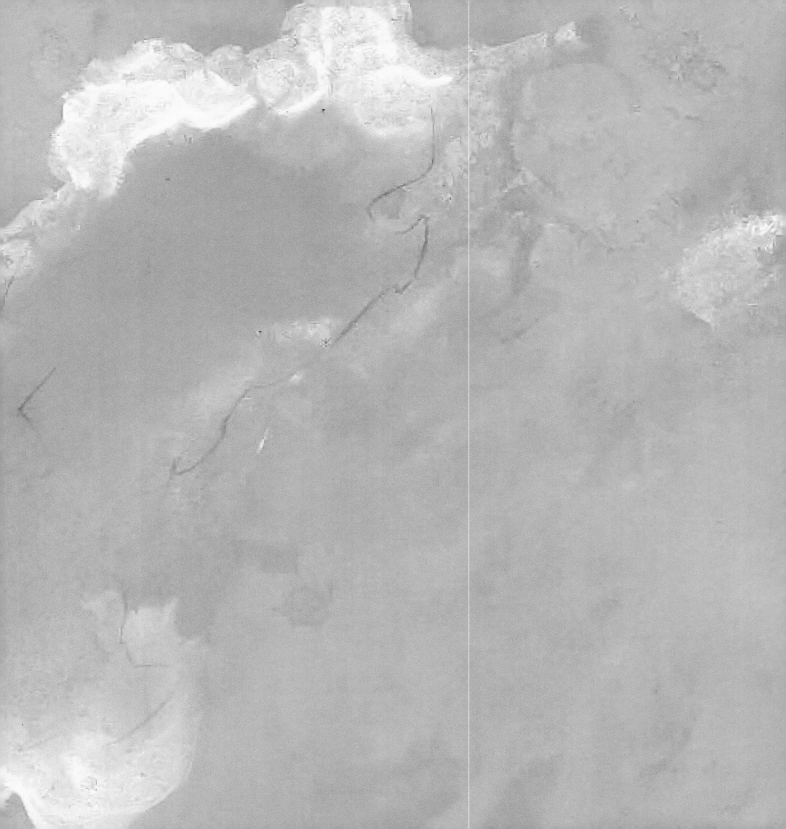

Sammy
in the Sky

Barbara Walsh

paintings by
Jamie Wyeth

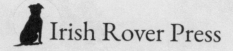

Irish Rover Press

His name was Sam.
But I called him Sammy.

He had black and tan colored fur, large brown eyes and a snout that could sniff three-day-old smells.

My dad said Sammy was the best hound dog in the whole world.

All I knew was that I loved Sammy and Sammy loved me.

Sammy was always at my side. He played house and doctor with me and never seemed to mind when I pulled a floppy pink bonnet over his ears or stuck bandages on his nose and paws.

At night, Sammy kept me safe.
He curled up on the floor by my bed, protecting me from bad dreams and the scary branches that scratched against my dark window.

If I woke up frightened, Sammy was there, his brown eyes watching over me.

Sammy always knew when I was sad. He'd nuzzle his nose in my lap and hand me his paw. Stroking his soft fur, I'd whisper, "I love you, Sammy."

Sometimes, Sammy made me laugh. When his belly was full, he would lie on his back, throw his legs in the air, and dance.

If my little sister and I blew bubbles, Sammy chased them, barking as he popped the tiny balloons with his paws.

I figured Sammy
and I would be
friends forever.
But the summer
Sammy turned
twelve, Daddy
found a bump on
Sammy's neck; it was as big
as a baseball.

The veterinarian told us Sammy was really
sick and there wasn't a medicine that could help.

When we got home from the doctor's, Daddy hugged Sammy. "You've still got plenty of fight, don't you, old hound dog?"

"We've got to love Sammy as much as we can," Dad said, "because he's not going to be with us much longer."

My father turned away so I wouldn't see the tears in his eyes.

I wrapped my arms around Sammy and held him tight.

We took Sammy to his favorite field and the beach, where he chased seagulls and other dogs. He still ran but not as fast and not as long as he used to.

Worn out, he collapsed on the sand.
"It's OK Sammy," I told him. "I'll take a rest with you. You're still the best hound dog in the whole wide world."

Sammy wagged his tail and licked my face.

Soon Sammy began limping and falling down when he tried to stand.

One morning he couldn't get up off the kitchen floor. Mom pulled me onto her lap. "Sammy's going to die soon," she explained. "When he leaves, his body will be like an empty shell, but his spirit will be everywhere – in the clouds, the fields, and the woods. All the good things about Sammy, like his love for you, will be yours to keep forever."

"I don't want Sammy to die!" I cried.

Then one night, Mommy and I came home and found Daddy holding Sammy.

Sammy gasped and wheezed, like he'd been chasing a squirrel for hours.

Daddy wrapped Sammy in a blanket, and we knelt by his side. I petted Sammy's head and kissed his warm nose. "You're the best hound dog in the whole wide world," I whispered.

Sammy's breathing grew slower and slower until it stopped.

"He's gone," Daddy said, his voice soft and strange.

Mommy held me close as Daddy carried Sammy to the backyard woods to bury him. "Goodbye Sammy," I cried.

The next morning, Daddy and I went for a long walk on the beach. I searched for Sammy in the sky. I searched and searched for a cloud that looked like Sammy. I looked for his face, his paws, and his big brown eyes.

"Can't Sammy come back?" I asked Daddy. "Just for a little while?"

Daddy shook his head. "You'll have to remember him in your heart," he said.

That night, I dreamt of Sammy. I felt his whiskers tickle my cheek, his cold nose nuzzle my hand. When the dawn light filled my room, I reached out to hug Sammy – but then I remembered he was gone.

My little sister didn't understand why Sammy went away. She shouted up at the sky, "Sammy, you come down here!"

"Maybe," she said, "If we get a really big ladder, Daddy can go get Sammy."

I knew there weren't any ladders that big.

As the summer days grew shorter, my chest stopped hurting when I thought of Sammy. My mother said it was time for a special celebration.

We took bottles of bubbles to Sammy's favorite field. We walked on the path where Sammy once ran, wagging his tail and sniffing scents. We told stories about the "best hound dog in the whole world."

Then we blew bubbles into the wind. They floated higher and higher toward a cloud that looked like a dog running in the sky. I could see its paws, floppy ears and tail.

"It's Sammy!" I yelled. "He's chasing the bubbles! Sammy's with us!"

"He'll always be with us," my mother said.
I stared up at the sky and shouted,
"I love you, Sammy! You're still the best hound dog in the whole wide world!"

For Eric, who taught his family

how to truly love a dog

B. W.

For all the dogs I have loved and lost

J. W.

Text copyright © 2011 by Barbara Walsh
Illustrations copyright © 2011 by Jamie Wyeth

All rights reserved. No part of this book may be reproduced, transmitted, or stored in an information retrieval system in any form or by any means, graphic, electronic, or mechanical, including photocopying, taping, and recording, without prior written permission from the publisher.

First edition 2011
This edition 2021

ISBN 978-1-7374813-0-0

The illustrations were done in watercolor.
This book was type set in EBGaramond
Page layout by Clif Graves of Hinterlandspress.com

Lightning Source UK Ltd.
Milton Keynes UK
UKHW051338050122
396631UK00002B/46